DIVINE
STRATEGIES
for
INVISIBLE
FIGHT

Femi Alaran

Published by Femi Alaran
British Library Cataloguing Data
A catalogue record of this book is available from the British Library

To obtain further copies or contact author:
Website: **www.LITWIC.org** Email: **contactus@litwic.org**
Printed in England

Dedication

"This is to you, Mom.
Thank you for always being there for me."

Acknowledgements

First and foremost, I would like to acknowledge and thank the Almighty God; He is the reason for my very existence.

I bless God for the countless men and women of God across the globe whose diverse ministries and gifts have benefitted me, right from my early days in Sunday school - the impact has been tremendous!

I would like to express my gratitude to all members of my family; and my friends for their understanding and support in completing this work.

I want to thank my editor and publisher for invaluable constructive criticism and friendly advice. Thank you for the excellent job of editing, proofreading, and publishing. It has been a long road, but we all made it.

I am deeply honoured in expressing my sincere gratitude to my fathers in the faith, for their knowledge and inspiration, namely: Pastor E A Adeboye, Bishop David Oyedepo, Dr. D K Olukoya, Derek Prince [late], Dr. Tony Evans, and many others. I am grateful, sirs.

Thank you
Femi Alaran

Contents

Introduction

'*Spiritual Warfare*' is a term that is commonplace in the body of Christ, often used as a one-liner that we hear thrown into prayers, sermons, and even songs.

The question is – do we really know what spiritual warfare is? And if we do, how does it apply to our lives?

Spiritual warfare is often spoken of in a 'spooky,' almost super-stitious tone. Perhaps this is because of the stories or testimonies that we have been exposed to. Maybe they are too far from our own 'reality.' For the average minded man – this is not surprising.

The spiritual world poses a mystic, airy-fairy, cosmic, and often doubtful existence. We only have to look around us to see the effect of the spiritual world on the physical world.

Think of a man who goes to work, receiving a pay-cheque at the month-end. After cashing the cheque, he walks down to the local grocery store, points at a packet of cigarettes, which is clearly labelled "Smoking kills," and requests that the shop attendant sell it to him. Like a skilled puppet master, the enemy hides behind the scene, while allowing his presence to be felt.

Jesus healed a lady who had been 'bent over' for eighteen years. A spirit of infirmity bound her. She may have visited many chiropractors in her day, seeking healing for her debilitating condition. Unknown to her, this condition was part of a symphony created by the 'piper' behind the scenes (Luke 13:11-13).

A lack of awareness of the realm outside our five senses (the spiritual) gives the enemy an added advantage as it's challenging to conquer what you don't know exists.

Spiritual warfare, like any warfare, is characterised by two or more forces in opposition to each other. The opponent or enemy to you as a child of God is the devil. You must be clear about who the enemy is. You cannot afford to have any ambiguity on this matter. This book deliberately refers to the devil as the enemy because, in warfare, it is crucial that we are objective – and remember that the devil is not on your side.

The enemy has perfected his strategies. His mission is to kill, steal, and destroy (John 10:10). Every Christian is expected to fight the war against the kingdom of darkness. The moment we surrender

our lives to the Lordship of Jesus, we're enlisted in the Lord's army, for the *"... reason the Son of God appeared was to destroy the devil's work."1 John 3:8*, and *"...the creation waits in eager expectation for the children of God to be revealed" Romans 8:19.*
The battleground has been shifted from heaven to the earth. Victory in spiritual warfare begins by putting on the right armour. Clarification on the dress code has been emphasised - the full armour of God in Ephesians 6:14-17,

"14 Stand firm then, with the belt of truth buckled around your waist, with the breastplate of righteousness in place, 15 and with your feet fitted with the readiness that comes from the gospel of peace. 16 In addition to all this, take up the shield of faith, with which you can extinguish all the flaming arrows of the evil one. 17 Take the helmet of salvation and the sword of the Spirit, which is the word of God."

No one can wage a successful warfare campaign against the enemy without having some form of training and plan for victory. David understood the importance of wearing the right armour, hence rejecting the armour of the king when it was offered to him (1 Sam. 17:38-40)

The objectives of this book are to:

- Introduce the reality of spiritual warfare
- Emphasise the importance of putting on each fragment of the armour of God
- Elaborate on the victory we have in Jesus

Finally, friends, we must possess the right perspective as we engage in warfare against the enemy. We are fighting 'from victory,' not 'for victory' (Colossians 2:15). Although our victory is specified, the kingdom suffers violence, and only the violent take it by force. We are not to be ignorant regarding the devices of the enemy. David said, *"Blessed be the Lord my strength which teach my hands to war, and my fingers to fight" Psalms 144:1*

My prayer is that you discover the strategies needed to overcome whatever challenges of life you are facing in Jesus' precious Name.

CHAPTER 1

Hide and Seek

"For our struggle is not against flesh and blood…"
Ephesians 6:12

Most adults have played 'hide and seek' as children. The objective of this game is simple, to find all hidden participants. As part of the game plan, nominations are made to seek their friends from their hiding places. The friends, on the other hand, have engaged their best efforts to hide in obscure places.

Like the children's game, evil spiritual forces hide in people's lives in places where their victims cannot easily detect them. The victim commonly seeks for solutions in every area possible - sadly incapable of explaining the situation that has befallen them. Such unexplainable plights are subsequently given a name or title. Such names are often long, complicated, and unpronounceable. No matter how sophisticated the terminology, we cannot make these forces disappear!

Nothing pleases a bully more than a victim who will not fight back or defend himself. It provides the bully with an adrenaline rush that perpetuates his behaviour, knowing that he will get away with it. The spiritual forces often operate like bullies and will continue to have a field day until they are resisted (James 4:7).

Spiritual warfare is the same as physical warfare, except the enemies are invisible. No leader surrenders his territory without a fight; equally, the enemy also won't surrender his gained territory without contending.

The good news is that we are fighting 'from victory' and not 'for victory,' "…having disarmed the powers and authorities, he made a public spectacle of them, triumphing over them by the cross" Colossians. 2:15. To wage a successful war against the enemy, we need proven tactics and time-tested strategies. A proverb says, *"Strategy without tactics is the slowest route to victory. Tactics without strategy are the noise before defeat"* [Sun Tzu, 2012]

A one-dimensional approach to the challenges of life gives the enemy an added advantage. If we keep throwing natural solutions at spiritual challenges, expecting them to go away, we will only get frustrated when tangible results are not seen. Since we cannot bury our heads in the sand like the ostrich, we must fight until we possess the gates of our enemy.

AREN'T WE OVER SPIRITUALISING THINGS?

All life flows from the spirit, and a body without a spirit is dead (James 2:26). If you believe in the existence of God and Him as the Creator, you must also believe in spirits. Spiritual things are more real than physical and natural things that we can touch, smell, or taste. The influence of the spiritual realm on our physical life can be seen in the story of Job. A conversation took place between God and Satan, and in one day, Job lost all that he had (Job 1:8-10)

During the earthly ministry of Jesus, He performed many miracles, and He would often cast out impure spirits behind the scene before the actual healing took place.

An example is the healing of the boy with seizures. Jesus rebuked the impure spirit, saying, *"You deaf and mute spirit, I command you, come out of him and never enter him again"* Mark 9:20 -27, resulting in total freedom for the boy.

I want to make the distinction between angels and demons. Angels are ministering spirits, often depicted as having wings and do not seek to possess a human body, and demons are bodiless spirits desperate for a body to manifest. The story of the mad man of Gadarenes shows just how desperate they can be. Imagine a legion of impure spirits possessing one man (Mark 5:1-12) Friend; we are not over spiritualising things. The realm of the spirit is the source of all things, and I, therefore, purport that the spiritual realm is indeed more 'real' than the physical world that we live in.

WE ARE AT WAR!

Many Christians still adopt a halfhearted attitude toward life. The wicked are doing more wickedly, and evil is on the uprise daily. A good army General finds a way to motivate his soldiers for every conflict by keeping the focus on the objective of the war. As humorous as it may sound, I believe the day we accept Jesus as our Lord and Saviour, we become enlisted in God's army, and like good soldiers, we must fight to defend our heavenly nation.

I have listed a few reasons why I believe, as Christian soldiers, we must keep fighting and not give up.

1. We must fight to take possession of our inheritance in Christ.

"See, I have given you this land. Go in and take possession of the land the Lord swore he would give to your fathers to Abraham, Isaac, and Jacob and to their descendants after them." Deuteronomy 1:8

The land of Canaan was promised to Abraham and his descendants by God. The land became their inheritance the moment God spoke. It took the warrior leader in Joshua to lead the children of Israel to possess their inheritance. Until we get violent with the enemy, our possessions will remain intact in his hands. We can weep, groan, and moan, but it doesn't change the enemy's mind about releasing what belongs to us.

Imagine, on Judgment day, God playing a video recording of how you lived your life in comparison with how He planned it. Due to your refusal to fight, you notice that there are huge discrepancies between His plan and how you lived your life. You may question this; like the rich man in the story of Lazarus (Luke 16:19-31), the scriptures say it is appointed unto men to die once and after this is the judgment (Hebrews. 9:27). In other words, there are no second chances. Therefore, we must fight to possess what belongs to us.

Imagine, on Judgment day, God playing a video recording of how you lived your life in comparison with how He planned it. Due to your refusal to fight, you notice that there are huge discrepancies between His plan and how you lived your life. You may question this; like the rich man in the story of Lazarus (Luke 16:19-31), the scriptures say it is appointed unto men to die once and after this is the judgment (Hebrews. 9:27). In other words, there are no second chances. Therefore, we must fight to possess what belongs to us.

2. We must fight to avoid being victims of spiritual theft

"The thief comes only to steal and kill and destroy" John 10:10

Every conflict has an objective, spiritual warfare is no different, and your place in eternity is the enemy's objective. He will use any means possible to achieve his aim. His interest does not lie in material possessions, and he uses them as bait to trap, or as a means to inflict harm. Since he knows his fate concerning eternity and where he is going, material possessions are frankly useless to him! (Matthew. 25:41). He is willing to trade the riches of the world for your allegiance to him. In other words, sell him your soul and lose your place in eternity.

Any valuables left unguarded, including salvation, will be stolen. The enemy simply lies in wait, like a predator for the most opportune moment to pounce on its prey. The scripture says, *"...if the good man of the house had known what hour the thief would come, he would have watched, and not have suffered his house to be broken through." Luke 12:39*

Friends, you must not lose your passport to heaven. You cannot afford to be stranded. The world will fade away with all its glory. Our priorities need to be in order, and we must hold fast to spiritual things, for they can be slippery (Hebrews. 2:1). Therefore, fight the good fight of faith.

3. We must fight to complete our assigned task

For the builders, every one had his sword girded by his side, and so buildeth" Nehemiah 4:18

I believe we have all been created for a purpose and knowing this, the enemy will attempt to do two things with regards to your assignment. He will try to stop you from discovering the purpose for which you are created; failing at that, he will do all he can to stop you from fulfilling your purpose. He knows that the fulfilment of your assignment is the destruction of his kingdom here on earth!

He often uses psychological warfare, which usually comes in the form of discouragement, i.e., the poisonous tongues of men. The scripture records the account of Nehemiah and the Jews who were being discouraged from completing their vision of rebuilding the broken wall of Jerusalem. Sanballat and Tobiah were the agents used during the days of Nehemiah. They cursed, insulted, and made a joke of the efforts being made by the men, intending to discourage them from completing the work (Nehemiah. 4:3). When they saw that their words didn't have the desired effect, they planned to attack physically. The likes of Sanballat and Tobiah still exist in the world today. We must remain defiant in the face of our distractors, most importantly, develop 'immunity' to their poisonous tongues. It is then that we can declare boldly like Zerubbabel, *"The hands of Zerubbabel have laid the foundation of this temple; his hands will also complete it. Then you will know that the Lord Almighty has sent me to you." Zechariah. 4:9*

We can learn a lot from the plight of Nehemiah. He did not handle the attack against him mono-dimensionally. He posted guards to hold back the physical threat and engaged in prayer to hold back spiritual attack *"…we prayed to our God and posted a guard day and night to meet this threat" Nehemiah 4:9* The guards were ready to fight; this should be the case for every serious builder. One hand must be on the plough and the other clenching the sword – a clear indication of the readiness to fight. God is committed to the fulfilment of our destiny. He will do His part, putting the 'super' in our natural once our natural effort is complete, thus making us supernatural. He infuses the 'extra' in our ordinary to make us extraordinary. In all of this, we must be responsible.

4. We fight to preserve the next generations

It is common practice for founders of multinational companies to preserve the posterity of the company by drafting in their children or grandchildren into their business. An example is Ford Motors Company, which has its fourth generation within the organisation. It is believed that the children will always look out for the best interest of their parents, maintain the traditions, and preserve their parental legacy. Jesus did the same for His disciples:

"Simon, Simon, Satan has asked to sift all of you as wheat. But I have prayed for you, Simon that your faith may not fail. And when you have turned back, strengthen your brothers." Luke 22:31-32

Jesus' work of salvation would have been a futile waste if He had failed to replicate Himself in His disciples, enabling them to propagate the message of salvation to the world. Peter was a soft target for the devil, but Jesus secured his destiny by praying for him. In other words, He fought the devil on his behalf. Our good works and successes are incomplete, except we can replicate them in future generations.

Jesus said, *"Very truly I tell you, whoever believes in me will do the works I have been doing, and they will do even greater things than these because I am going to the Father." John 14:12.* I thank God for my praying mother, who spent countless hours in the 'prayer room' to secure the destiny of her children.

5. We fight because it is what we are meant to do

"All that is necessary for the triumph of evil is that good men do nothing," How accurate is this saying by Edmund Burke? I wrote a scriptural equation, using the following scriptures:

"Thou, therefore, endure hardness, as a good soldier of Jesus Christ." 2 Timothy 2:3, "For this purpose the Son of God was manifested, that he might destroy the works of the devil" 1 John 3:8b, and "...as he is, so are we in this world." 1 John 4:17

And so:

2Timothy 2:3 + 1 John 3:8 + 1 John 4:17 = We must Fight, for this is what we are commissioned to do.

As soldiers of God, we're equipped for the establishment of God's Kingdom here on earth. Since there are no demilitarised zones and no one can serve two masters, we must fight, for this is what we are called to do. The devil is not passive. He is going to and fro, the length and breadth of the earth seeking whom he may devour. He will continue to have a field day as long we permit him to do so.

"Behold, I give unto you power to tread on serpents and scorpions, and over all the power of the enemy: and nothing shall by any means hurt you" Luke 10:19

Power is ineffective without use. I enjoy boxing because it is a very technical and highly engaging sport. It requires a careful study of your opponent, discerning his strengths and weaknesses. A momentary lapse of concentration will allow your opponent to land the knockout punch that can end the bout in a matter of moments, even though you may have been ahead on points. Sometimes Christians get discouraged in a spiritual match, especially when they cannot see the effect of their prayer on the enemy.

Staying with boxing as an illustration, please note that every punch a boxer lands on his opponent earns him points. He cannot always tell the effects of his punches on his opponent until the end of the bout; that is, of course, if he hasn't already been knocked out before the final bell. Do you realise that we can tell the effect of our punches on our opponent? The secret lies in the Bible, *"...for greater is he that is in you, than he that is in the world." 1 John 4:4.*

If the greater One is inside you, then your punches must be more potent than those of your enemy, though he might pretend that your punches have no effects on him. If you maintain the momentum and continue to land your punches in your prayers and fight against the enemy, you will eventually knock him out. Force remains the only language the devil understands, and until we engage in it, he will not relinquish his stronghold.

Belt of Truth

"Stand firm then, with the belt of truth
buckled around your waist..."
Ephesians 6:14

The first piece of armour is the belt of truth, which is the foundation of our spiritual armoury. A belt is multi-functional, primarily to keep our clothing in place and to prevent our nakedness from being exposed, thereby causing shame. Without a belt around our waist, we stand the chance of tripping over our clothing. If we neglect the belt of truth in our war against the enemy, we stand a high probability of being exposed and ridiculed.

In our readiness for spiritual warfare, the belt is comparable to a cowboy's gun holster or swordsman's scabbard, which is used to hold the offensive weapon against the enemy. Without the belt of truth fastened around our waist, we will lack the credibility to fight the enemy who is the master of deception. To secure the belt of truth around our waist means to bind ourselves with Christ, who is the Author and Finisher of our faith. He protects us against every collision or harassment of the enemy. Knowing who we are and to whom we belong gives us the boldness to stand firm in the face of opposition and remain on course for our destination.

THE MASTER OF DECEPTION

"...When he speaketh a lie, he speaketh of his own: for he is a liar, and the father of it." John 8:44

All warfare is based on deception [Sun Tzu, 2012] since no man can outsmart the devil in evil; the best way to overcome him is by operating in the truth. Any man attempting to play the enemy at his game is only setting himself up for a mighty fall. The enemy knows how to tailor lies to suit his agenda. Deception isn't false at every point, but with a few minor adjustments here and there, it can contain some element of truth, which will seem plausible to the listener. I can recall a simple statement made by my head-teacher many years ago when I was in secondary school. He said to us during a morning assembly, "If you imagine God on top of a mountain, and you at the bottom of it, the various religions of the world are different paths to God, so there is no perfect religion." The statement sounded harmless and logical, with a high tolerance for all religions. However, it violated the truth from the scriptures. Jesus said, *"I am the way and the truth and the life. No one comes to the Father except through me," John 14:6.* If I had no knowledge of the truth, I would have been hooked on the devil's lies.

Like every good sales assistant, the enemy makes people think he is doing them a favour while selling them something they don't need. Consider the Biblical account of the fall of man in Genesis chapter 3. Eve was convinced that *"becoming like God"* would solve all her challenges; perhaps she felt lonely as Adam was often away tending the garden of Eden. The truth is that she was made in the image and likeness of God (Genesis 1:27). The 'sales speech' began with a harmless conversation, until the serpent's fangs 'entered into her skin' to release his deadly poison.

During my education at Business school, my Economics professor shared his knowledge of how to start a subscription business for a magazine that provided information on the direction of the stock market. He said that you begin by having 100 potential members whom you have scouted from any source. You send 50 of your potential subscribers a list of stocks, stating that the direction of the stock you have handpicked will go up. Send the remaining 50 potential subscribers a list indicating the stock prices will go down, knowing fully well that the stock prices will either go up or down. For this illustration, we assume that the stock prices did go up as predicted to the first 50 potential subscribers. Repeating the process, you divide the 50 people you have correctly predicted the direction of the stock prices into two halves. You will send the first 25 a list of stock prices claiming it will go up, and the remaining 25, the stock prices will go down. By the end of the 2nd week, there will be 25 out of 100 people who believe that you can predict the direction of the stocks you have handpicked. You then send a letter to them, claiming information such as this is very valuable, and that it could make them millionaires overnight. In the letter to them, you also inform them that they can receive more useful information from you by subscribing to your magazine for a small annual fee. Now imagine the baseline number was not just a hundred people, but a hundred million people - the profit would be astronomical!

This strategy is similar to that which the enemy uses to lure his victims into a trap. He doesn't tell them an outright lie; that would be too easy to detect. Instead, he begins by telling the truth 'mixed' with some lies. Once the person is hooked onto the bait, then he can rail them in like a fisherman. The easiest way to outsmart the devil is to obey God entirely.

THE CONSTANT TRUTH

"Jesus Christ is the same yesterday and today and forever." Hebrew 13:8

During my University education, I taught mathematics to secondary school students as a part-time job. Throughout the lessons, I observed that my students often struggled with questions containing multiple variables. To help them solve their calculations, I told them to start by looking for the constant - the known variable, and work their way from there; a simple yet effective strategy.

Life, in many ways, is like a mathematical question with many variables. However, we may not be able to express our difficulties with arbitrary letters and figures; we often deal with multiple factors at a time, which can be challenging, even for the most organised person. For any mathematical calculation to be solved, there must be an aspect of it that must hold true no matter what manipulation takes place with other numbers. For any challenges in our lives to be resolved, there must be an aspect of it that holds true no matter how volatile the environment gets. Just as I have asked my students in the past, I have also asked Christians, "What do you know to be true, irrespective of your current situation or present circumstances?" Often, they respond by saying, "God is good," to this, I add, "not only is God good, but His Words are also true, a constant in our variable world." His Word has been tried seven times in fire, which makes it flawless, so we are not experimental guinea pigs for trial and error to see which part of His Word works or not! *"Forever, oh, Lord thy word is settled" Psalms 119:89*

Times change, seasons change, but the Word of God remains the same throughout all generations. This gives us hope and assurance that irrespective of the challenges we face, we are secure based on the truth of the Word of God. Like a ship at sea, God's Word is our anchor that stabilises our position and movement, keeping it from being tossed to and fro by the waves of the sea. Our knowledge of the truth keeps us steady in every storm of life.

TIGHTEN YOUR BELT

"Be alert and of sober mind. Your enemy, the devil, prowls around like a roaring lion looking for someone to devour" 1 Peter 5:8

Our Christian journey is also comparable to our experience on an aeroplane. The captain announces to the passengers, "fasten your seat belts," and advises that they keep them fastened throughout the flight. The airline attendants go around, ensuring all the seat belts are fastened, knowing the danger or accidents that could occur if the seat belt is left unfastened. It is dangerous for any Christian to attempt to take off in the air and fly at a high altitude without having their lives well tucked under the belt of truth.

As soldiers of Christ, to tighten our belts indicates readiness for battle, while a loose belt shows we are off duty. As Christians, we are never off duty; the scripture says, *"No one serving as a soldier gets entangled in civilian affairs, but rather tries to please his commanding officer." 2 Timothy 2:4.* If indeed we aim to please God, then we must be alert at all times, for the enemy is continually going around seeking for prey to devour. It is the norm for young men these days to let their trousers fall below their waistline, a fashion trend called 'sagging.' It actually impedes movement and their ability to run. By not tightening the belt of truth, you might find yourself 'sagging' spiritually. It leaves you in an awkward situation with no option but to compromise your beliefs and ethical standards, thereby losing your effectiveness as an ambassador of Christ. Life, as they say, is a jungle, may we never be easy prey for the enemy in Jesus' Name.

STRENGTHENED BY THE TRUTH

"For we can do nothing against the truth, but for the truth" 2 Corinthians 13:8

You may have observed that weight lifting trainers and bodybuilders at your local gym often wear a large belt around their waists. These belts are to support their backs and prevent them from sustaining severe injuries while lifting heavyweights. The belt around their waists can be likened to the belt of truth, which is a central piece in our spiritual armour, and not a fashion accessory! The belt acts as overall support for our entire armour, just like the backbone of the body. The enemy seeks to undermine and destroy our credibility, which leaves people second-guessing every word we speak both in private and in public.

Lying always backfires. It is like keeping multiple copies of the same file in different locations without any version control. The integrity of the document is compromised, and it is difficult to know which is the most up to date version. The truth inspires confidence and courage, which is unparalleled. It strengthens your armour, allowing you to move freely without fear. The irony of life is that it takes an extremely long time to build a reputable character, but in a split second, it can all be lost.

Let me share a story with you: I once went to the grocery store with a friend to buy two loaves of bread. Arriving at the shop, we met people with whom we exchanged pleasantries. While we talked with the people, the storekeeper packed the loaves of bread in a bag for us, and we left the shop without paying. On our way home, I noticed that there were more coins in my pocket than I expected. I said to the friend with me, "we haven't paid for these loaves of bread." He replied, "Don't worry about it," but I insisted we go back and pay, even though we were almost home. We returned to the shop to pay for the loaves of bread.

The incident took place some years before my ordination as a Pastor. The friend who accompanied me that night could have stood as a witness against me if he was called, saying if I am unfaithful by not paying for loaves of bread, how can I be trusted to manage God's finances? I view it this way - I would have sold my integrity for two loaves of bread like Esau, who sold his birthright for a meal. Personal integrity is required for a walk with God; although we might congregate together in a place for worship, we all stand as individuals before God. Hence, we all wear the belt of truth individually.

CHAPTER 3

The Breastplate of Righteousness

"…having on the breastplate of righteousness"
Ephesians 6:14

The second piece of our spiritual armour is the *"breastplate of righteousness,"* which is a protective cover for the chest area. The chest cavity is home to significant organs of the body, including the heart. The heart is more than just a muscle that pumps blood around the body and keeps us alive. The word 'heart' can have different meanings depending on the context in which it is being used.

The state of a man's heart can be described by his physical, emotional, and spiritual wellbeing. A healthy heart will typically mean a healthy body, while a weak heart will result in a fragile body. The heart can also be used to describe a man's personality. You may have heard phrases, such as "he is big-hearted," or "he is hard-hearted." The indicated tells us the kind of person with whom we are interacting.

A man's belief and perspective on life tells us the condition of his heart, *"for out of the abundance of the heart the mouth speaks."* Luke 6:45. Ultimately how we feel about ourselves is determined by our heart; hence the scriptures tell us to guard our hearts with all diligence for out of it flow the issues of life (Proverbs 4:23)

Our relationship with God is established on the condition of our hearts. We also see in the Bible that the heart is used to describe the spirit of man. We cannot relate to God with our flesh for He is Spirit; it takes Spirit to spirit connectivity to forge a meaningful relationship with Him. At Redemption, our belief was not based on the physical organ in our chest, but rather our 'spirit man' acknowledging the Sovereignty of God and confessing with our mouths that, "Jesus is Lord." (Romans 10:9-10). This makes the heart a strategic point for the enemy to attack, for it holds not only the key to our physical wellness but also the spiritual victory.

David cried out to the Lord, *"Create in me a pure heart, O God, and renew a steadfast spirit within me."* Psalms 51:10 Just as the body cannot function effectively with a weak heart, we cannot have a cordial relationship with God with an unclean heart. The condition of our heart dictates our standing in God; God searches the heart to reward every man according to their deeds. (Jeremiah. 17:9-10).

If our hearts are unprotected, we are left vulnerable to the enemy who unremittingly seeks for an opportunity to attack us with his fiery arrows of depression and doubt. *"The spirit of a man will sustain him in sickness, but who can bear a broken spirit?" Proverbs 18:14.* Unless a man's spirit is wounded or defeated, there is always hope for victory.

THE BREASTPLATE OF LOVE

"…let us be sober, putting on faith and love as a breastplate…" 1 Thessalonians 5:8

Our breastplate of righteousness must be forged in the 'indestructible steel of love' for it to be able to withstand the piercings of the enemy. Love keeps our hearts tender toward God and men. The absence of love in our hearts results in us becoming insensitive to the leading of the Spirit of God. When our hearts become drugged with insensitivity to the Holy Spirit, we grow spiritually ambushed by the enemy. God forbid that we ever end up as 'spiritual prisoners of war' (SPOW).

Our actions and, indeed, reactions must be motivated by love so that we don't reduce our acts of righteousness to mere eye service. Jesus warned that we should not portray our acts of righteousness as to be 'men-pleasers,' but as 'God-pleasers' with a genuine interest in the wellness of others so that we don't forfeit our reward (Matthew 6:1)

While a single premeditated blow to the chest of a soldier can be fatal, it follows that when our actions are motivated by love, we don't suffer heartbreak, even when the recipient doesn't reciprocate in a like manner to us.

Love is one of the most significant forces of all time. Our hearts are connected to our emotions - the enemy can use emotions to hurt us or those close to us. We must protect our hearts with the unyielding force of love so that we can withstand all that the enemy throws at us (1 Corinthians 13:13).

TIMING AND THE BAIT

"…each person is tempted when they are dragged away by their own evil desire and enticed" James 1:14

Every skilful hunter knows the importance of bait in enticing unsuspecting prey into a trap. The enemy we war against is a skilful hunter, who seeks an opportunity to pounce on his prey. Timing plays a crucial role in our aspiration for righteous living. Many have become victims of circumstance and peer pressure by merely being in the wrong place at the wrong time.

The Bible's narrative of David in 2 Samuel depicts this truth: *"In the spring, at the time when kings go off to war, David sent Joab out with the king's men and the whole Israelite army. They destroyed the Ammonites and besieged Rabbah. But David remained in Jerusalem" 2 Samuel 11:1.* This single event led to a rollercoaster of other actions that smeared David's impeccable record as the 'shepherd boy' who rose to the throne as king. He took the 'bait' of the naked woman innocently taking her bath, and he ended up being an adulterer and a murderer (2 Samuel 11:14-15)

The enemy is an astute tactician. His 'tailor-made' temptations are craftily designed to suit each individual whom he seeks to entrap. [Sun Tzu, 2006] makes this assertion:

"If your opponent is of choleric temper, try to irritate him. If he is arrogant, try to encourage his egotism. If the enemy troops are well prepared after reorganisation, try to wear them down. If they are united, try to sow dissension among them" [The Art of War, 2012].

We must not be ignorant of the enemy's devices. He is known to tempt extravagantly, with a red carpet overlaying a pit filled with spikes. One of our daily prayers should be, "Lord order my steps so that I don't walk into the trap of the enemy."

Some time ago, I was at the Barber's shop to watch a soccer game. I met a man who shared his life's story with me. He had worked as a manager of a warehouse company for some years and went on to explain the following unforgettable story.

One morning, in the early hours, while at work, he received an urgent phone call from the hospital. He was told his attention was needed at the hospital as his pregnant wife, who was due to deliver their baby, was experiencing complications. He was required as a signatory to consent to the intended emergency Caesarean section. Due to the urgency of the call, he left work early but signed his timesheet as though he had left work at the stipulated closing time. The story became even more complicated as he explained that only a few hours later, he was informed that the warehouse was robbed! Being the duty manager, the owners of the warehouse demanded an explanation. No matter how hard he pleaded innocent, and even though he was at the hospital at the time of the robbery, his signature on the timesheet indicated otherwise - consequently, he was sacked and blacklisted.

After listening to this man's story, I asked myself several questions, such as "...would an hour's wage affect his standard of living?" And, "...if he had signed his timesheet correctly - would his employers have stopped him from going to the hospital if he had called them?"

As it happened, this man had been separated from his family for two years. Mostly, he had missed out on the new baby's life due to difficulty in securing suitable employment. The financial burden that was presented when the new baby arrived was too much for him to bear, resulting in his migration to another nation to find employment to sustain his family. What a great price to pay all for an hour's wage? The enemy is seeking people to devour; may you be exempt from that list in the precious name of Jesus!

SELF-RIGHTEOUSNESS

"Two men went up to the temple to pray, one a Pharisee and the other a tax collector. The Pharisee stood by himself and prayed: 'God, I thank you that I am not like other people robbers, evildoers, adulterers or even like this tax collector. I fast twice a week and give a tenth of all I get.' But the tax collector stood at a distance. He would not even look up to heaven, but beat his breast and said, 'God, have mercy on me, a sinner.' I tell you that this man, rather than the other, went home justified before God. For all those who exalt themselves will be humbled, and those who humble themselves will be exalted." Luke 18:10-14

A self-righteous person substitutes God's righteousness through Jesus, with works without the help of the Holy Spirit. Self-righteousness has its roots in pride, and it gives the enemy easy access to puncture the breastplate of righteousness. He knows that in all our self-righteousness, we are like filthy rags (Isaiah 64:6). The Bible says, *"…not having mine own righteousness, which is of the law, but that which is through the faith of Christ, the righteousness which is of God by faith" – Philippians. 3:9*

The Pharisee displayed arrogance and a sense of superiority over the tax collector because he felt assured of his works as a qualification before God. He had forgotten that it is God who sees in secret and rewards openly (Matthew 6:4). Only the righteousness that comes by faith in Jesus strengthens spiritually.

At times, doing right gains us no instant gratification, sometimes we almost feel like giving up, especially when those who don't live by God's law and standards seem to prosper. Jacob said, "*So shall my righteousness answer for me in time to come…*"*- Genesis 30:33*

The testimony of a young man illustrates this scripture. This young man worked as a male model and was called for a modelling job in a different part of the country. He had just enough funds to get him to the destination, with the hope that he would be paid for the job promptly. As God would have it, he was told that the payment for the job would be sent to him at a later date! So, with no cash in his pocket, he was stranded, unable to return home. He sat down in the hotel lobby, contemplating a way out of this predicament.

While thinking, an older gentleman walked past him and suddenly walked back to him and asked the question, "Are you the son of Mr. X?" The young man replied, "Yes." The gentleman began to narrate, "I know your father, he is a good man, and he allowed me to fetch water from his tap many years ago." Willing to repay the act of kindness shown to him by the young man's father, the man dipped his hand into his pocket and gave the young man some money. The amount was more than enough to cover his transportation fee back home. The young man did not reap the fruit of righteousness, but that of his father. Some of the seeds of righteousness we have sown today will outlive us, be watchful.

RIGHTEOUSNESS EMPOWERS

"The LORD is far from the wicked, but he hears the prayer of the righteous" Proverbs 15:29

Righteousness is the soil in which great faith grows, and without faith, it is impossible to please God. We can have the seed of faith, but if we have no soil to plant it in, our seed could go to waste. Just as the earth protects the seed from being food for the birds of the air, so does our righteousness preserve our faith and belief in God, even when it looks more profiting to do otherwise.

Righteousness produces power in prayer and grants us an audience with God as a matter of urgency, for *"the effectual fervent prayer of a righteous man availeth much" - James 5:16*. The patriarch Abraham negotiated for the life of his nephew - Lot, using righteousness as a bargaining tool (Genesis 18:22-32). It is possible to make a lot of noise in the prayer room and get no results when righteousness is out of place.

Righteousness gives credibility to our prayer. We can learn a lesson from the life of King Hezekiah, who was told he was going to die, immediately he turned his face to the wall and cried unto God, reminding how he has done that which is good in thy sight (2 Kings 20:1-5).

Righteousness creates boldness, keeping the rhythm of the heart steady at the sound of the doorbell; knowing whatever is on the other side of the door is for good. *"...the righteous are bold as a lion" Proverb 28:1.*

Righteousness thoroughly frees us from the condemnation of our past, for old things have passed away, and all things have become new. We are new creations in Christ, not through our works but by faith in Christ Jesus.

CHAPTER 4

The Gospel of Peace

*"…with your feet fitted with the readiness that comes
from the gospel of peace,"*
Ephesians 6:15

Life is an obstacle-laden marathon. For an Olympic athlete, the correct footwear can make all the difference between being a champion and a mere participant. As spiritual athletes, the right shoes protect our feet, keep us comfortable, balanced, improves our performance, and provides the needed support to complete the race.

The journey of life is riddled with booby traps. To ensure the soles of our feet are protected, we must ensure that our feet are firmly fitted with the readiness that comes with the gospel of peace. The enemy tries to offer us 'alternative' spiritual footwear other than those prescribed for 'Christian soldiers.' Imagine a soldier wearing a pair of high heels to a battlefield! Such would surely hinder his responsiveness and agility, making him a soft target for the enemy. The gospel of peace is essentially the ministry of reconciliation, which is an evangelical ministry. This is the great commission given to us by Jesus to "go into the entire world, and preach the gospel to every creature," Mark 16:15. This is an 'offensive' campaign against the kingdom of darkness. It is safe to say that no king will relinquish his crown and throne without a fight. The devil and his hosts will not give up the people they wish to dominate without a fight.

The right set of shoes will also keep us from developing blisters. I had a conversation with a friend some years ago. He told me that he wished Jesus would come that day, especially since there had been much talk about the return of Jesus for so long, and He was yet to return. I responded by asking him when he got born again. He informed me that it was the year 2000; I went on and explained that if Jesus had come back in 1999, he would have missed heaven! He looked at me strangely. Soul-winning is a matter of urgency and should not be taken lightly.

EXCUSES

The "readiness that comes from the gospel of peace" shows our responsiveness to the mandate of our Commander in Chief. Our modern-day, hectic lifestyles often mean we have more things competing for our time than we can ever manage; this habitually hinders our ability to evangelise and share the gospel. But we always seem to 'make time' for things that are of lesser heavenly priority. There is no demilitarised zone in the war against the kingdom of darkness. You are either on God's side or not!

I have often heard people say, "I don't know what to say to people when I go out to evangelise." The story of the Samaritan woman at the well with Jesus teaches a lesson about evangelism. She went back into the town and told everyone of her encounter with Jesus - that is evangelism in its simplest form. (John 4:28). Evangelism is simply telling people what the Lord has done for us. Paul says, "...preach the Gospel, not in cleverness of speech, that the cross of Christ should not be made void." 1 Corinthians. 1:17. All we have to do is tell people what the Lord has done for us.

DIVIDE AND RULE

"Every kingdom divided against itself will be ruined, and every city or household divided against itself will not stand." Matthew. 12:25

For the soldiers of Christ to present a formidable front against the enemy, there must be unity within. Unity is a virtue that grows from the stem of peace. The practice of 'Divide and Rule' is an old strategy of warfare. It works by undermining a stronghold from within by creating internal conflict. A scriptural example is found in the narrative of three nations that allied to fight against the children of Israel. The Bible records that God defeated their armies by setting them up against one another until they destroyed each other (2 Chronicles 20:21-23). The enemy also copies this strategy of warfare and applies it to Christians.

He tries to break up our stronghold from within. One of the ways he applies this warfare strategy is trying to isolate us from God's presence. He tries to manipulate our thoughts and emotions by connecting imaginary dots in our minds pointing at and accusing God, trying to make Him directly or indirectly responsible for our challenges. Like Martha said, "Lord, if you had been here, my brother would not have died," John 11:21, or Job's wife, "Do you still hold fast to your integrity? Curse God and die!" Job 2:9.

Once we lose the backing of our greatest allies, our stronghold is divided, and we are left to our weaker self.

The second way the enemy applies this warfare strategy is to break up our alliance with others. The scriptures say, "... if two of you on earth agree about anything they ask for, it will be done for them by my Father in heaven," Matthew 18:19. The enemy fears the power of unity, for he knows, "one will chase a thousand and two shall put ten thousand to flight," Deuteronomy 32:30, Peace breeds unity, and in unity, God commands His blessings (Psalms 133). The devil will do all he can to destroy the harmony that we have within so that we don't harness that great power. No doubt living peacefully with others is sometimes a mammoth task considering the varying human personalities that we come across daily. Still, the scriptures admonish, "If it is possible, as much as depends on you, live peaceably with all men, so that the devil will have a foothold on us," Romans 12:18.

THE UMPIRE OF THE HEART

"...the peace of God, which transcends all understanding, will guard your hearts and your minds in Christ Jesus." Philippians 4:7.

Peace acts as the umpire of the heart-protecting us from distractions, especially when the storm of life is raging all around us. A man fighting an internal battle will have very few resources or strength to fight external ones. An area where we are often under siege is our self-perspective. The desire to look good in the eyes of others has driven many to misbehave simply to 'fit in.' Our self-esteem fluctuates based on the acceptance of others, thus losing peace with ourselves. We operate like spiritual junkies looking for a quick fix; this gives the enemy an added advantage. He knows a soldier with low morale won't be able to fight optimally. Have you noticed how quickly you change your mind over a matter after a good night's rest? When a man's heart is unsettled, he finds himself making irrational decisions because, frankly, all common sense goes out of the window! If you allow worrying to take over your heart, you will lose the protective cover that comes with God's peace.

The fear of the 'unknown' has caused many to stumble and others to backslide, especially when faced with difficult situations. It is crucial to understand that the peace of God is not the absence of challenges, but rather an assurance that He is with us in all situations. Jesus said, "… In the world you will have tribulation; but be of good cheer, I have overcome the world." John 16:33. The good news is that the umpire of life is on our side, He is the Prince of Peace, so no matter how bad the storm is outside; it is safer to remain in the boat with Jesus. He assures us that He won't allow more on us than we can bear (1 Corinthians. 10:13). So, when the enemy hurls thoughts of discouragement against us, we have peace that we can handle it. Our spiritual shoes of the gospel of peace keep us from being moved, despite the devil's schemes. Peace is linked to all areas of our lives. It affects not just our physical wellness but also infringes on our prosperity and sensitivity to the leading of the Holy Spirit. These areas are strategic points in spiritual warfare.

HEALTH IN PEACE

"A heart at peace gives life to the body" Proverbs 14:30a

Some severe illnesses have been linked to the lack of peace: anxiety, depression, high blood pressure, hypertension, and malnutrition, are just a few. When our hearts lack peace, our minds are restless, and then the devil is allowed to roam freely in our thoughts. He plants the seed of unbelief, which he uses to rob believers of God's healing, blessings, or even His plan for their lives. Job said, "What I feared has come upon me; what I dreaded has happened to me. I have no peace, no quietness; I have no rest, but only turmoil." Job 3:25-26

Like our tongues, our thoughts need to be tamed and controlled. When we are robbed of peace, our bodies lack the motivation and strength to complete any task. By worrying, none of us can add a day to the length of our lives. Have you ever wondered why God hasn't taken any action to remove the burdens from our shoulders when He knows we sometimes feel overwhelmed? The answer is simple; although He is the Almighty, He is still a 'gentleman' and will not interfere in man's affairs - except when He is invited (Psalms 115:16). He has the power to break the door down, but still, He knocks! We have carried the burden for too long, "Cast all your anxiety on him because he cares for you," 1 Peter 5:7. We have a father who cares for all our needs.

PROSPERITY IN PEACE

"I have been deprived of peace; I have forgotten what prosperity is" Lamentations 3:17

Peace is closely linked to prosperity and productivity. If we are to prosper, then the peace of God must saturate our lives. Even the most brilliant mind will struggle to be productive under duress or in a hostile environment. Imagine being under siege, where everyone is running for their lives. All economic theories or principles will be utterly useless; then, the only principle applicable will be survival.

A key reason why Israel prospered during the reign of King Solomon was that the nation fought no battles. The king's mind could think progressively on how to move the nation forward economically (1 Chronicles. 22:9). He was not worried about the welfare of soldiers on the battlefield, or how to raise taxes to fund a war campaign. The nation's tourism industry blossomed; people came from far and near to behold the magnificence of Solomon's kingdom. Can you imagine going on vacation to a war-torn country?

GUIDANCE IN PEACE

"And thine ears shall hear a word behind thee, saying, this is the way, walk ye in it, when ye turn to the right hand, and when ye turn to the left." - Isaiah 30:21

It will be difficult for us as Christians to isolate the "still small voice" of the Holy Spirit - the inner witness and assurance when peace is absent from our hearts. The absence of peace in our hearts is an indicator that our focus is shifted from God – we are reminded, *"for He keeps them in perfect those whose mind stays on him."* Isaiah 26:3

The absence of peace in us will lead to multiple voices speaking to our hearts. These strange voices often lead us astray or into a trap. If the enemy becomes successful in breaking our communication with the heavenly quarters by disrupting the peace in our hearts, he leaves us in isolation.

Many people cannot see beyond a few metres via the natural eye, but the Holy Spirit helps us to see and know which step to take – as well as the precise timing, to secure our victory in battle. The Holy Spirit is often symbolised as a dove; hence peace is a requirement and not optional for a successful war campaign against the enemy.

CHAPTER 5

The Shield of Faith

"Above all, taking the shield of faith, wherewith ye shall be able to quench all the fiery darts of the wicked."

Ephesians 6:16

Christianity is called 'the faith' - this makes Faith the most visible and prominent part of our spiritual armour. It's a lifestyle that exemplifies Christ. The shield of Faith is primarily for our protection, but it can also be used as an offensive weapon in spiritual warfare, by speaking Faith-filled words at the enemy.

"Fiery darts" are like long-range assault weapons used in combat without coming face to face with the enemy. Archers fire from a distance, hundreds and possibly thousands of arrows into the air to weaken the opposition. Such indicators can be used to describe the challenges we face as Christians; they are sent to undermine

41

us or discourage us from forging ahead. When a Christian puts down his shield of Faith and relies on his ability and personal experiences, he leaves himself vulnerable to the manipulation of the enemy, who incidentally is far more tactically superior in warfare. The shield of Faith is a central piece of our spiritual armour that we must not leave behind for whatever reason, whether day or night.

INTELLIGENCE GATHERING

Faith is being knowledgeable. Knowing God's will in a given situation assures us of victory. David enjoyed flawless victories in his numerous battles - his secret was that he sought to know God's will before he engaged in any battle. Zeal doesn't equate to knowledge. Paul wrote, "For I bear them record that they have a zeal of God, but not according to knowledge," Romans 10:2. It is good to be zealous, but a lack of knowledge offers the enemy an opportunity to exploit us as a loophole in a security system.

During the days of Moses, he sent out spies to explore the land of Canaan; he said, *"Go up through the Negev and on into the hill country. See what the land is like and whether the people who live there are strong or weak, few or many. What kind of land do they live in? Is it good or bad? What kind of towns do they live in? Are they unwalled or fortified? How is the soil? Is it fertile or poor? Are there trees in it or not? Do your best to bring back some of the fruit of the land." Numbers 13:17-20.* He did not rely on zeal and then negate the art of intelligence gathering; this scripture verse teaches the basics of spiritual warfare. In warfare, we don't approach the enemy without first collating an intelligence report regarding the enemy we are about to fight. Failure to do this will result in the wrong tactics being deployed. Being Christian does not exempt us from the necessary due diligence before we fight.

You don't have to be good with numbers to get a good grade in mathematics; you merely have to understand the worked example (Romans 15:4). It is quite ironic how quickly we forget the problem-solving skills we learnt in school. Once we leave school, especially when we are confronted with difficult situations, we seem to become quickly overwhelmed and allow ourselves to be disillusioned. Since there is nothing new under the heavens, we must seek for worked real-life examples - just as we would for questions in an examination. We can draw strength from the testimonies of others as a means to strengthen our Faith. Faith draws its virtue from knowledge.

HEARING

"…faith cometh by hearing, and hearing by the word of God" Romans. 10:17

Words have reproductive capabilities, like seeds. Once planted, they take root, germinate, and grow. Positive words empower and energise; negative words demoralise and rob people of their confidence. The enemy is a patient adversary; he plants negative seeds in our mental database —often in our childhood years or youth when we're more susceptible to what we hear. He then sits patiently and seeks to reap the harvest in our adult years. A man who has suffered verbal abuse as a child will generally grow up to have low self-esteem. Negative words are cancerous; they spread uncontrollably to other areas of our lives. Jesus warns, "Take heed what you hear…" Mark 4:24. Our ears are like windows into our soul; they play a significant role in the development of our Faith. The soul functions like a database, which we often consult before making decisions. We must have the right information in our database. Paul admonishes us to update our database with the truth of God's word (Romans. 12:2)

DO NOT DROP YOUR SHIELD

"While men slept, his enemy came and sowed tares among the wheat, and went his way" Matthew. 13:25

A commonly used tactic of the enemy is to attack when we least expect it. *"While men slept"* implies a time when we have our guard down, a time we feel safe and secure, especially when we are around friends and family. It's the times when we put down the shield of Faith and feel restful. The enemy seeks for moments like this to attack. We see a classic example in the life of Jesus, He called Peter *"the devil,"* just after He had praised him for having such an outstanding revelation. Why? Peter was being used as a stumbling block to the fulfilment of His destiny (Matthew. 16:23). Jesus' guard was always up.

Let me, once again, share a similar experience; I was at the barber's watching a football match. During the half time interval, the group engaged in a conversation about marriage and families. Suddenly, someone said to me, "What if I can't have children?" Immediately I raised my shield of Faith; I replied, "It can never happen to me!" I hadn't finished my statement before a lady replied angrily to my words, "Don't say that, you don't know if you will be able to have children." I replied again, "It can never happen to me."

Interestingly no one bothered to ask me why I had so much confidence that I was going to be fruitful in marriage. They were more interested in criticising my statement than in finding out the truth I had discovered about fruitfulness. If I had allowed their words to sink into my soul, the enemy would wait to reap a harvest in the area of fruitfulness in marriage.

REVELATION

"…it is given unto you to know the mysteries of the kingdom of heaven, but to them it is not given." Matthew 13:11

Revelation is exposure to the mysteries of the kingdom of heaven. Revelation gives life and meaning to the letters of the scriptures, *"for the letter kills, but the Spirit gives life," 2 Corinthians. 3:6.* The engine of our Faith is turbo-boosted when the letters of the scriptures come to life in our hearts. If Christ has revealed Himself to us as the Healer, our Faith should be receptive to receive healing. I came across this startling revelation some years ago; this skyrocketed my Faith. I read in the book of Matthew, where Jesus said, *"…All power is given unto me in heaven and in earth," Matthew 28:18.* The Holy Ghost inspired me, and I asked, "If Jesus has all power in heaven and on earth, what power does the devil have?" The definition of the word "all" includes the following; entirety, everything, whole, complete. On that day, it was as if light entered every dark corner of my heart, I could call the devil's bluff, and I saw him (and see him) henceforth as a toothless bulldog. The scriptures say, *"…having disarmed the powers and authorities, he made a public spectacle of them, triumphing over them by the cross," Colossians 2:15.* The devil seems to harass people who do not know who they are in Christ.

"The kingdom of heaven is like treasure hidden in a field. When a man found it, he hid it again, and then in his joy went and sold all he had and bought that field" Matthew 13:44

Revelations are like buried treasures that can change a man's fortune in an instant but require a diligently executed search to unearth them. Once found, they must be guarded like trade secrets; this gives a sense of value and worth to them. It impacts the lives of those who find them, as well as leaving a lasting legacy through subsequent generations.

PRAYING

"The apostles said to the Lord, "Increase our faith!" Luke 17:5

The development of Faith is a lifetime journey. Our faith increases as we progressively tackle more and more opposition. Faith is not a theory or philosophy; we don't see reason or hypothesise Faith! It is action in a particular direction. Just as a bodybuilder doesn't develop his muscles by theories and speculative assumptions, we cannot build our Faith by reclining in our favourite comfortable chair.

The prayer point, "Lord Increase my faith," is perhaps one of the essential prayer points we all need to pray. We will all be faced with a moment of weakness when we desire to stay in our comfort zone. Nevertheless, we cannot experience the miracle of walking on water if we choose to remain in the boat. When we ask God to increase our Faith, He provides us with an opportunity to exercise our Faith. As we know, Faith without works is dead. No soldier receives a medal of honour without fighting battles.

CELEBRATE SMALL VICTORIES

"...the Lord that delivered me out of the paw of the lion, and out of the paw of the bear, he will deliver me out of the hand of this Philistine." 1 Samuel 17:37

These were the words of David before he fought Goliath. He recalled the various moments of deliverance the Lord had performed in his life; these served as great faith boosters before he faced Goliath. I also apply this in my personal life, by often reaching for my diaries and recounting God's marvellous acts in my life, reassuring me that my tomorrow will be nothing less than God's best!

Learning to celebrate past victories - no matter how small or insignificant they may appear, increases our capacity to face challenges. The lion and bear conquered by David were no comparison to the giant called Goliath - but the actual recollection of those victories strengthened his Faith to face the challenge ahead. (1 Samuel 30:6)

There will be times in life when nobody will be around to encourage you - your pastor, family or friends will be nowhere to be found (1 Samuel. 30: 4-6). Learning to celebrate small victories ignites your Faith. I encourage Christians to maintain a diary of God's wondrous acts in their lives; this is particularly useful when you feel as though there is no one to turn to. Reading and recounting does strengthen your Faith and keeps the flame of encouragement burning.

FELLOWSHIP WITH OTHER SAINTS

"Not forsaking the assembling of ourselves together, as the manner of some is; but exhorting one another: and so much the more, as ye see the day approaching" Hebrews 10:25

At the height of the Roman Empire, they conquered nations with their military might and experience. They had the tactics to outmaneuver any other army. The bow and arrow were the most advanced weapons used, allowing nations to do significant damage from a distance. However, the Roman soldiers, would use their shields to form a rectangular shape as a roof that resembled a modern armoured tank. It enabled the soldiers to advance into the enemy's territory despite the onslaught of arrows.

Likewise, as Christians, we can keep advancing through life's challenges if we join our shield of Faith with other likeminded Christians. Like a spiritual armoured tank, we will become an unstoppable force, bulldozing every enemy along the way. One shall chase a thousand, but two shall chase ten thousand, and *"…if two of you on earth agree about anything they ask for, it will be done for them by my Father in heaven," Matthew 18:19.* This is the mystery of unity and the joining of our Faith.

EXERCISE YOUR FAITH

"We having the same spirit of faith, according as it is written, I believed, and therefore have I spoken; we also believe, and therefore speak" 2 Corinthians. 4:13

When we speak God's Word, we are holding up the shield of Faith and preventing penetration from the fiery darts of the enemy. The battle between David and Goliath was decided by words before they had any physical contact. (1 Samuel 17:42-48) Child of God - do not hesitate to speak the word when words contrary to your Faith are being spoken. In other words, do not approach your giant with your mouth closed! If David had contacted the giant with his mouth closed, he would have lost the battle, because the pronouncement of the Word of God saturates our shield of Faith, with the "water of the Word" that extinguishes the flames of fiery arrows.

Paul was a man of tremendous Faith; the scriptures record that God performed extraordinary miracles through his hands. He exercised his Faith regularly by preaching the gospel, that is, sharing the gospel as a means to use his Faith. Spreading the gospel allows us to put the words we have learnt to work. Jesus said, "*…we shall lay hands on the sick, and they shall recover*" *Mark 16:18*. Faith empowers us to do the impossible, for, with God, all things are possible.

Every moment of sinking in our lives begins when we doubt God's character. Circumstances will change, people will fail us, and we might even disappoint ourselves. However, God is constant - He will never change. He is ever dependable. He will not deny Himself.

CHAPTER 6

The Helmet of Salvation

"...take the helmet of salvation..."
Ephesians 6:17

The head functions as the central processing unit of a computer. It determines our actions, reactions, and all that we do. It is the seat of our mind and consciousness; this makes the head the most valuable part of the body and the prime target of the enemy. In most developed nations, laws have been passed that make it mandatory for all cyclists to wear helmets to prevent serious injury to the head in the event of a collision. Similarly, there is a heavenly decree that makes it mandatory for all Christians to wear the helmet of salvation, to prevent serious injuries in our spiritual battle against the enemy. The mask of salvation protects our heads from all assaults of the enemy via the blood of the Lamb.

The head serves as an entry point to the rest of the body; it houses the mouth, nose, ears, and eyes. It is a common practise within the Christian community for ministers to lay their hands on other ministers as a means of transferring the anointing, which flows from the head to the rest of the body. If a man's head were missing from his neck, there would be no point of entry for the anointing into the rest of the body. When the head receives the anointing, the helmet of salvation protects it, preserves, and seals it.

THE STRONGHOLD OF THE MIND

"Casting down imaginations, and every high thing that exalteth itself against the knowledge of God, and bringing into captivity every thought to the obedience of Christ" 2 Corinthians. 10:5

The city of London in England - is renowned for being very cosmopolitan. It is home to a diversity of nationalities, ethnic groups and cultures, and typifies a melting pot in all of its most accurate senses. The city is divided into boroughs to allow for proper management of resources to meet the needs of the people. The city has a legally employed mayor who is responsible for the affairs of the city. While he can claim to be legally in charge, there are people of the underworld in different boroughs across the city who are also in charge of their vicinity. These people often operate as gangs and engage in turf wars.

Now let us imagine our minds as a city, with many boroughs within it. As Christians, Jesus is the sole government that should reign in our minds. But the truth is, there are 'localities' of our mind still occupied by the enemy through various influences – examples of such include traditions, past experiences, and false or wrong doctrines – this is by no means an exhaustive list. These 'strongholds' operate like the mafia - sabotage, extortion, rigging, and all manner of lawlessness. If these strongholds are not served an eviction notice - they will hinder the best of God for us.

The solution is to renew our minds; this process includes the eviction of the strongholds within us, by conforming our thinking pattern to that of Christ (Romans. 12:2). It is not a one-time event but a lifetime process. Sanctification describes this process more accurately; it must prevail until the mind is entirely subject to the government of Christ.

STINKING THINKING

"Finally, brethren, whatsoever things are true, whatsoever things are honest, whatsoever things are just, whatsoever things are pure, whatsoever things are lovely, whatsoever things are of good report; if there be any virtue, and if there be any praise, think on these things."
Philippians 4:8

Thoughts are compelling - they shape our lives, actions, reactions, and ultimately, our destiny (Proverbs 23:7). The mind is where the battle is fiercest; a quote by Lao Tzu says, *"Watch your thoughts; they become words. Watch your words; they become actions. Watch your actions; they become habits. Watch your habits; they become character. Watch your character; it becomes your destiny."* The mind processes thousands of thoughts daily, which gives the enemy plenty of opportunities to mount an attack with impure thoughts.

It is crucial to note that the enemy cannot read our minds and can only attempt to corrupt our thoughts. He has a good knowledge of how we will react to temptations when we are presented with them. Our facial expressions and body language often give a clue to what we are thinking. He then invades our minds with thoughts that can strategically take advantage of us in our weak moment.

Jesus warned us about our facial and bodily expressions - not to give 'clues' to the world as to what is going on within us. He used the scenario of fasting to teach this important principle - when we fast, we should not appear before men as though we are fasting. For a man who is fasting, the ideal temptation is food. Fasting is a spiritual exercise which must be done in secret, and the reward is seen openly (Matthew 6:16-18)

GLORY

"When his lamp shone on my head and by his light I walked through darkness!" Job 29:3

A man's head carries his glory. The wise men from the East saw Jesus' star, and they came to worship Him (Matthew. 2:2). This light of glory is a constant threat to the kingdom of darkness - they will seek to extinguish the light before it manifests.

I want to share the testimony of a young man, who after completing his Bachelor's degree, had a strange dream. In his dream, he saw himself having a strange haircut in a familiar place, by an unfamiliar person. At face value, this dream was insignificant since it is common practise for a young man to get his haircut regularly, but if a matter lingers in the mind for too long, we may encounter it as a dream (Ecclesiastes. 5:3a). As time passed, everywhere this young man applied for employment, he was turned down. Could this be a coincidence? A rational person would probably ask whether he engaged in pre-interview research, or whether his CV was up to scratch. The line of inquiry could also lead us to ask whether he fitted the personality specifications, and, of course, whether he was fully qualified for the post. May I remind you that spiritual things are not based on technicalities. Honestly, the questions are good, but nothing changed for this young man until he engaged in warfare prayers.

The scriptures record the lifetime of Samson, a great man who did extraordinary things through the Spirit of God. But he lost his strength when his hair was shorn from his head (Judges 16: 17 -19). His eyes were gouged out, and he became subject to ridicule. Some mistakes are correctable with time - but others leave us with permanent scars in our minds and emotions. Sometimes there are also physical scars. Samson's hair grew back with time, and his strength returned, but his sight was not restored. It is our responsibility to guard our light against being extinguished by the enemy.

IDENTITY

An inward choice of the mind precedes every action. A key variable in our decision-making is our identity. Once we forget who we are, it becomes easy for the tempter to lure us into sin. The tempter said to Jesus, *"…If you are the Son of God, tell these stones to become bread." Matthew 4:3* The irony of this temptation is that Jesus was publicly announced in the previous chapter as the Son of God (Matthew 3:17), yet the tempter questioned Him about his identity. Have you wondered why? If Jesus had fallen at this first hurdle of forgetting who He was and what He was sent to the world to do, He would have succumbed to the other temptations easily.

In contrast, is the Biblical record of the fall of man: the tempter said to Eve, *"For God knows that when you eat from it your eyes will be opened, and you will be like God, knowing good and evil." Genesis. 3:4-5* Eve wasn't aware that she was made in God's image and likeness,"she took the bait and fell into sin.

"Therefore, if any man be in Christ, he is a new creature: old things are passed away; behold, all things are become new" 2 Corinthians 5:17

Often new believers struggle with their identity. There is often a tussle in their minds between who they were and who they are at the new birth. The enemy senses this struggle as a strategic point of entry into the life of a new convert. He bombards the mind of the new convert with records of the past as bait to lure them back into their old ways. If he is successful in creating doubt about our identity - he will successfully lure us into sin.

THE HELMET OF HOPE

"...for a helmet, the hope of salvation" – 1 Thessalonians. 5:8

Imagine a situation where a pre-recorded football game featuring your favourite team is playing, and you plan to view the game with friends who are fellow supporters. Now it just so happens that you are privy to the final score of the game, and your team won, while your mates are none the wiser. I am sure you will agree that there will be a difference in your behaviour and those around you during the game – right? Because you know the final score and they don't. Any decisions the referee makes against your team won't bother you because you know who wins! Even when the opposition looks well organised in their defence, you will be as cool as a cucumber because of what you know.

Let's say that the first half of the match ends with the opposition in the lead, and as the second half begins, the challengers score their third goal within the first ten minutes! By now, your fellow club supporters will be fully persuaded that your team is going to lose the game. Imagine the match continues until the last ten minutes of the game, by which time all around you have lost hope. However, you remain calm – then suddenly, your team scores two goals in quick succession in the 83rd and 85th minutes of the 90-minute game. In the 89th minute, your team scores the equaliser! You all rejoice – fully content with a draw –as this means that at least you manage to score a league table point. Then - interestingly there are four minutes added to game time, and suddenly your team is awarded a penalty in the 93rd minute - this seals the fate of your opponents, and your team is victorious!

While everyone was on the edge of their seats, they would wonder why you hadn't seemed too bothered about the rollercoaster experience that had ensued. Well, of course, you wouldn't be bothered because of your foreknowledge.

Hope works similarly to the foreknowledge of the outcome of the soccer match. Hope is a deep conviction of the outcome of an event that is yet to occur, based on prior knowledge. The scriptures provide us with the foreknowledge of events about the world to come, with the helmet of hope on our heads, we have peace in every storm (John 16:33).

Can you envisage how miserable life would be without hope? Basically, without hope, life becomes meaningless. Picture this; we would rise from our beds every morning without any motivation and sleep at night without anything to look forward to the next day. With hope, there is always light at the end of every dark tunnel.

Hope is our tremendous motivator in this somewhat volatile world.

As Christians wearing the helmet of hope, we can walk around with our heads held high. Our perspective on life becomes different from that of the world; we finish from victory, not for victory, for, in the end, we will always win (Colossians 2:15). When you find yourself perpetually in fear of what the future holds, you merely need to obey God in the present. The future is simply a harvest of the seed sown in the present. No one plants a good seed and reaps a bad harvest (Galatians. 6:7). Hope produces holiness; hope produces perseverance; in the end, we will exchange our warrior's helmet for a crown of righteousness like Paul. Therefore, we must keep our eyes on the finish line (2 Timothy. 4:7-8)

CHAPTER 7

The Sword of the Spirit

"...the sword of the Spirit, which is the word of God"
Ephesians 6:17

The Word of God is the ultimate weapon of war for every Christian. It is an indestructible double-edged sword that has been tried and tested, making it the faultless choice for both defensive and offensive warfare against the enemy. The Holy Bible is unlike any other book. It is an extension of God's authority on earth, for where the Word of the King is, there is power (Ecclesiastes.8:4)

The military operates a highly organised hierarchical structure that allows for the flow of orders to move from the top to the lower ranks at the bottom. A Sergeant cannot give an order to a Colonel and expect the Colonel to obey him, as the Colonel is not subordinate to the Sergeant. However, a Colonel will follow instructions from a General, who is his superior – even if that instruction is passed via the Sergeant. The power of the scripture extends beyond the physical realm; principalities and powers will not obey the words that we ordinarily speak, but they are bound to obey the Word of God in our mouths. It makes the Word of God the most valuable weapon a Christian possesses.

ON GUARD

"...Always be prepared to give an answer to everyone who asks you to give the reason for the hope that you have. But do this with gentleness and respect," 1 Peter 3:15

All Christians are expected to be on 'their guard,' for our adversary, the devil, is going around seeking whom he may devour. I would like to share another of my experiences with you – this time, I was out of the house doing my customary evening prayers. I reached my favourite spot, and while pacing up and down praying, I was approached by two police officers in their patrol car. They introduced themselves politely and proceeded to question me about my movements, which looked strange to them. I introduced myself as a resident of the neighbourhood and explained that I was praying. One of the officers asked me about the Bible, while his colleague checked the system to verify my identity. The officer quizzed me about the book of Matthew chapter 6 and Exodus chapter 20, respectively. I answered his questions systematically, telling him about the Lord's Prayer and the Ten Commandments.

I then proceeded to ask him what he believed in. He told me he was a Freemason. We conversed on Freemasonry, and I shared my knowledge on this practice in an unbiased manner. He was surprised that I wasn't ignorant, nor did I show blatant prejudice on the matter. I was completely comfortable and secure in my identity as a Christian (and I remain so). I explained that I was not ignorant of what goes on in the world. We must note that being a Christian doesn't make us naive.

If I had failed to answer the police officer's questions correctly, he might well have doubted my authenticity as a Christian, and possibly even developed a wrong view of Christians. If I was ignorant of the topic of Freemasonry, he could have lured me into the occult by selling me a fantasy. Be on your guard; life's examination has no timetable or prior warnings.

HANDLE SKILLFULLY

The Word of God, like every weapon of war, must be handled with skill and care. I believe that an untrained soldier armed with a weapon is more dangerous than an unarmed enemy. One of the greatest services a soldier can perform for his battalion is to become acquainted with his weapon until it becomes an extension of his body. The temptations of Jesus graphically show us how He parried the attack the enemy lunged at Him. He repeatedly told the tempter, "it is written," knowing that the power of the scriptures cannot be resisted (Matthew. 4:1-11). The scriptures can often be made to say almost anything. If care is not taken, the truth can be twisted. The tempter tried to turn the Word of God by attempting to confuse Jesus about what is written. We must therefore know and understand for ourselves what is written; the Bible says:

*"Study to shew thyself approved unto God, a workman that needeth not to be ashamed, rightly dividing the word of truth"
2 Timothy 2:15.*

Using the scriptures correctly requires proficiency, obtainable only from diligent studying. Consider these two scriptures found in Matthew 5:44 and Matthew 11:12, *"...love your enemies and pray for those who persecute you,"* and *"And from the days of John the Baptist until now the kingdom of heaven suffereth violence, and the violent take it by force."* If both scriptures are read in isolation, it could lead to misinterpretation and, therefore, erroneous application.

OUR LIGHT

The old hymnal by John H. Sammis says, *"When we walk with the Lord in the light of His Word, what a glory He sheds on our way!"* In the dark, it is thought that a driver can only see about six feet ahead without the aid of the headlamps. However, with functioning headlamps in place, he can travel and navigate thousands of miles across the country, avoiding potholes and other hazards on the road. When we have the headlight of the Word of God shining in our hearts, we can 'navigate life' to our God-ordained destination.

Light comes in varying degrees of intensity, just like the wattage of a light bulb. The more of His Word that is in you, the greater the intensity of light you emit. The power of light from a household light bulb cannot dispel the darkness in a stadium. Demons often fell prostrate at the appearance of Jesus without Him even uttering a word. Why? The light being emitted was too intense for them. (Mark 5:6)

The scripture tells us that *"The entrance of thy words giveth light; it giveth understanding unto the simple" Psalms. 119:130.* But who are the simple? The simple are those who believe anything, they are gullible, and they float on every wave of doctrine presented to them. (Proverbs.14:15a) When the enemy knows we are susceptible to this 'simple' mindset, he uses this as an avenue to penetrate our spiritual armour by offering fables as substitutes to the Word of God. Be assured that in the same way that no artificial light can compare to the light of the sun, no substitute can compare to the glory that comes from God's Word. It is our antidote against the darkness.

POWER-PACKED

The Boxing Federation categorises fighters according to different classes of weight, these range from featherweight to heavyweight.

A boxer in the featherweight division cannot compete with a boxer in the heavyweight division. The sheer size and strength of the heavyweight boxer are sufficient enough to intimidate any featherweight boxer. Such a bout would be deemed unfair and a mismatch. Likewise, in spiritual warfare, God will not allow us to encounter more than we can bear. In other words, if we are classified as spiritual featherweights, we will not be allowed to take on a heavyweight challenge. Be rest assured that whatever you are facing at this moment, you can handle it (1 Corinthians. 10:13).

Visualise your prayer sessions as a boxing bout, with each prayer point as a jab, or punch to the enemy's jaw. The more jabs and punches you deliver on target, the greater your chances are of knocking him out. The depth of His Word determines the force of the punch thrown within you. *"For greater is He in that is in you than he that is in the world" I John 4:4*. If the greater One resides in you, then the power of your punches must be greater than those of the enemy. You must not entertain the thought that your punches are not affecting the enemy, merely because you can't see him ascertain the impact you are having on him. You can be sure that he is suffering more pain than you can imagine. So, keep fighting and don't let down your guard.

For a boxer to be successful in the ring, specific vital attributes are required:

Concentration - A professional bout lasts twelve rounds. A boxer may be winning eleven rounds of the bout unanimously, but a split second of poor concentration can leave him open for the enemy to land the knockout punch that will overturn the bout in his favour.

Consistency – It is essential to maintain momentum until the end of each spiritual bout. Imagine a boxer landing a powerful punch on his opponent, and then going to sit at his corner? It would allow the opponent time to recuperate from the effect of that punch and to come back like a wounded lion seeking revenge. *"Better is the end of a matter than the beginning thereof, and the patient in spirit is better than the proud in spirit." (Ecclesiastes 7:8)* We must maintain momentum until the end.

Endurance - Mental toughness and resilience are pivotal. Since the Bible states, *"He that endures until the end shall be saved," Matthew 24:13*, we must be prepared to go the distance. In those twelve rounds of the boxing match, if a boxer falls in one round and can get up, there is hope that the bout might turn in his favour. There are twelve calendar months in a year; it doesn't matter how many times you have been knocked down, there is still hope for you, as long as there is life. You can land that knockout punch that will leave the enemy flat-out on the floor, so don't give up!

You are fighting an enemy in the same weight class as yourself that you can handle. Don't be so scared that you allow the enemy to walk away with your championship belt. Get back in the ring - now! Take back your blessing, breakthrough, relationship, and health, and strike that demon back!

SPIRITUAL DIET

"Man shall not live on bread alone, but on every word that comes from the mouth of God" Matthew. 4:4.

Every athlete striving for the best must maintain a strict diet plan to stay in optimal physical condition. As Christians, we must subscribe to heaven's dietary plan to become spiritually vigorous. A balanced diet is essential to keep up our spiritual energy. God's word provides the balance that we need. The devil operates like a bully seeking those he sees as malnourished, for he knows they won't fight back. Though many appear outwardly healthy, it is sad to note that countless Christians are spiritually malnourished. If you find yourself always being picked on by the enemy, check your Word intake. Being spiritually malnourished makes the armour of God a burden, especially the shield of faith, because there is no internal strength to sustain it.

I would like to share the testimony of Derek Prince (1984) from his book, 'God's Medicine Bottle.' He was diagnosed with a rare skin condition, and after the doctors did all they could, he thanked them and returned home. Being a medical professional himself, he decided to read the Word of God after each meal he ate, just as he would if he was taking prescribed medication. Within a matter of months, his skin condition was not only gone, but there were also no visible scars on his skin that would imply he ever sustained a skin disorder!

WORD RESPONSIBILITY

"You are the light of the world," Matthew. 5:14

We all carry the responsibility to 'ignite fire' in each other. The decision was made the day we surrendered our lives to Jesus. Picture a room filled with seated people, each one holding a candle. If only one person's candle is lit, he can increase the illumination in the room by merely lighting the candle of the person next to him. And, so, the process continues until everyone in the room has their candlelit. The combined intensity of each candle will dispel and destroy darkness much more than only one person's candlelight.

"For the creation waits in eager expectation for the children of God to be revealed" Romans 8:19

The Christian life is one of responsibility. We must see to it that we light each other's candles, bringing enlightenment to each other with God's Word in us. We must guide against forces that try to snuff out our light or take our candle away. We cannot fight the enemy with human reasoning; this would be like going to a gun duel carrying a knife. We must bear the responsibility of making disciples of all nations. We are the light of the world!

CHAPTER 8

Pray Always

"Praying always with all prayer and supplication in the Spirit..."
Ephesians 6:18

Prayer is more than just expressing our heart desires to our Maker. It is a means by which we release unseen forces to do battle against the enemy. Many Christians find prayer a burdensome chore, primarily when they cannot associate their efforts with any tangible result. They would instead sing and dance, than pray.

Prayer remains a timeless and effective weapon in the mouth of any Christian. However, it seems unbelievers believe more in the power than believers do! Mary Queen of Scots is quoted to have said, *"I fear the prayers of John Knox more than all the assembled armies of Europe."* Prayer is more accurate than any intercontinental ballistic missile and more potent than all nuclear bombs put together. The enemy knows the power of prayer and will prevent anyone from discovering its true potential, including pretending that our prayers do not affect him.

Seeing results is a key motivator in our prayers - the enemy knows this too and will do all he can to withhold the answer to prayers of the saints. The scriptures tell the story of Daniel, who prayed for twenty-one days before he received the answer to his prayer, though the answer was sent from the first day he prayed (Daniel. 10:12 -14). By employing such delay tactics, the enemy has managed to trick many into believing that prayer doesn't work and then hijacked the answers to people's prayers in the heavens. Prayer is a means to ask, track, and receive delivery of solutions.

THE RESPONSIBLE FATHER

Jesus introduced God to us as our Father, not a cruel taskmaster who sits in heaven and expects everyone to do His bidding. As the Father, He is responsible for the well-being of His children. The scriptures say, *"Anyone who does not provide for their relatives, and especially for their own household, has denied the faith and is worse than an unbeliever." 1 Timothy. 5:8.* Would God deny the faith He enacted?

God can NEVER be intimidated by the size of our requests; neither is He overwhelmed by our persistent asking (John 16:24). When Nathan, the prophet, confronted David about his sin with Bathsheba, he said to David, *"I gave your master's house to you, and your master's wives into your arms. I gave you all Israel and Judah. And if all this had been too little, I would have given you even more." 2 Samuel. 12:8.*

I want to share another scriptural equation with you; this involves the following three passages:

"After this manner therefore pray ye: Our Father which art in heaven, Hallowed be thy name" Matthew. 6:9

"Which of you, if your son asks for bread, will give him a stone? Or if he asks for a fish, will give him a snake? If you, then, though you are evil, know how to give good gifts to your children, how much more will your Father in heaven give good gifts to those who ask him!" Matthew. 7:9 -11

"Anyone who does not provide for their relatives, and especially for their own household, has denied the faith and is worse than an unbeliever." 1 Timothy. 5:8

From these three scriptures, I can deduce:

Matt. 6:9 + Matt. 7:9-11 + 1 Tim. 5:8 = "I am a responsible God and Father. Ask of me, and I will give it to you."

HOW OFTEN SHOULD I PRAY?

The answer is simple, *"…men ought always to pray, and not to faint," Luke 18:1*. Knowing that life is warfare, and each day has its battles, we must reinforce our defence line and make it impregnable. Jesus prayed often,; He spent more time praying than He did attempt to solve the challenges that He faced. By virtue of this, He had tremendous success in His ministry. The reverse is the case of many; we spend more time attempting to solve problems than we do praying. The secret is this; the more time we spend with Him, the more of His glory we absorb, and whosoever that cannot withstand the glory of the Father cannot withstand us (Psalms. 114:7)

Another noteworthy testimony. A preacher prayed to God for a trailer home for himself and his family. He began praying to God for his needs in October 1998. A year later, in October 1999, a friend requested that he accompany him to a prayer meeting, while on their way, the friend asked if they could stop at an airport hangar - the preacher agreed. They both exited the car and went into a trailer home. They met a man who was known locally to be wealthy; he said to the preacher, "I heard you are looking for a trailer home." The Preacher affirmed this, and the wealthy man said to him, "look around you, does this trailer home meet your needs?" The man of God replied affirmatively with great joy. Then the wealthy man said, "It is yours in Jesus' Name." This is the first 'half' of the testimony - a further conversation with the wealthy man revealed something astonishing. He had bought the trailer home in October 1998, when the man of God began praying for one, but it had to go through refurbishment to the tune of $270,000.

While the preacher was praying for the trailer home, God was putting the finishing touches in place, and once it was complete, it was delivered. Perhaps you also have a need you have been praying about for a while now. Don't give up because the finishing touches are being added, and it will soon be delivered!

PRACTICAL STEPS

"...the spirit indeed is willing, but the flesh is weak." Matthew. 26:41b

Many Christians know the importance of prayers but find it difficult to pray; the flesh exercises dominance over the spirit. In such situations, the knowledge of prayer is not lacking, but the training of the flesh. You need to be aware that the flesh needs to be tamed and trained like a wild horse. For instance, many of us desire to pray early in the morning or late in the evening, but once we get into a comfortable position to pray, we fall asleep.

Most Christians, if not all, go through this phase in their spiritual development. Having gone through this phase of development myself, I would like to share some solutions that could help resolve the challenge.

Our physical posture can affect the energy our bodies generate. By kneeling at the bedside or lying on the floor while we are praying - especially after a day's work; we are offering the body the opportunity to drift into sleep. Consider walking around the room and praying out loud; this will engage not only the spirit but also the body. I must warn that we must be careful not to disturb our neighbours by doing so! You might also consider inviting a likeminded Christian for the prayer session, the scripture states, *"....one shall chase a thousand; two shall put ten thousand to flight," Deuteronomy 32:30.* The pair of you will serve as an encouragement to one another (Proverbs. 27:17). Finally, a splash of cold water on the face or a shower might help get the body in shape for prayers.

Let's face it - we sometimes get distracted while praying. There are two kinds of distractions, internal and external distractions. External distractions can be efficiently dealt with by finding a solitary place to pray like Jesus often did (Luke 5:16). Still, the internal distractions are slightly more challenging to deal with because this involves our minds. Although we can lock our doors, close our windows, and switch off our phones, our thoughts remain within us, and they can be running from pillar to post though our bodies are physically still. The ability to calm the mind varies from person to person, but the good news is that we can all develop the ability to shut out internal distractions. A technique that has helped me develop my focus in the 'prayer room' is to approach prayer dutifully. I often set out some time preparing for prayer with scriptures to go along with each prayer point - this stops my mind from wandering or running out of words. Each prayer point is like a 'to do' list that keeps me focused. I encourage all Christians to perform the duty of an intercessor while they pray. God is always seeking for intercessors, and your desired breakthrough might hinge on your prayer for others (Job 42:10)

Finally, we must all learn to exercise the gift of the Spirit - praying in tongues. Many times we do not know what we ought to be praying for and how we ought to be praying for it. But by praying in the spirit, we eliminate errors in our prayers. The Holy Spirit takes over our prayers.

I recall an instance some time ago, where I awoke in the middle of the night to go to the toilet. On my way back to bed, I strongly felt the need to pray, not sure what the prayer was for, and I had no pressing need. I decided to pray in tongues (pray in the Holy Spirit) - I prayed until I felt a release to go back to sleep. I awoke in the morning, only to be called by a friend who told me that a domestic incident had occurred during the night. Still, a timely intervention prevented the situation from escalating. I knew that this was due to answered prayers and the power of intercession at work (Ezekiel. 22:30).

THE EFFECTIVE PRAYER

"...the effectual fervent prayer of a righteous man availeth much."
James 5:16b

There are times we pray earnestly about something in our lives, but we can't understand why God is not answering us. Have you been there? I certainly have. One of the reasons is a breakage in communication between God and us. It will be impossible for God to answer a prayer He has not heard, no matter how many times we have repeated the prayer point. Sin doesn't only break our communication link with God. It destroys our spiritual armour from within. It can be likened to the fifth column leaving us vulnerable to the attacks of the enemy. We have firm confidence when sin is absent in our lives, *"whatsoever we ask, we receive of him, because we keep his commandments, and do those things that are pleasing in his sight." 1 John 3:22*

Praying without the Word of God is like holding a gun without any bullets in it. The enemy might just call your bluff too. The scripture provides the necessary firepower essential to subdue the enemy, and this is one of the reasons I strongly encourage Christians to spend some time in preparation before engaging in prayer. This 'prep' involves searching through the scriptures for relevant portions of the Word to back our requests. It will not only strengthen your request; it will also increase your faith, knowing that you are standing on the Word of the Lord.

"Howbeit this kind goeth not out but by prayer and fasting." Matthew 17:21

Fasting is one spiritual process that many Christians don't want to subscribe to. It is a means by which we suppress the influence of our flesh to heighten the sensitivity of our spirit to the Holy Spirit. It is an act of discipline and humility, for the flesh is prideful, and it will oppose all God centred activities. Have you noticed that, when it is time to pray, your body is reluctant, yet it sits quietly before a television set?

In the gospel, according to Mark, we see an incident of the disciples of Jesus struggling to cast out a demon from a little boy. They further noted that Jesus did this with ease right in front of them. When they asked Jesus why they couldn't cast out the demon, He told them, *"...this kind can come forth by nothing, but by prayer and fasting," Mark 9:29.* Fasting is essential, especially when you are dealing with difficult situations.

Finally, always remember to pray to the Father in the Name of Jesus.

CHAPTER 9

Stay Connected

"I am the vine; you are the branches. If you remain in me and I in you, you will bear much fruit; apart from me you can do nothing."

John 15:5

Having done all we know to do, we need the patience to wage a successful war campaign against the enemy. A simple way to eliminate murmuring and complaints is to engage in thanksgiving, praise, and worship. By doing so, we keep ourselves connected to the source, as we follow the protocol into His presence (John 15:5). It is sometimes easy to forget how far God has brought us, and the things He has done when we are faced with pressing challenges. Many times, we barge into God's presence demanding from Him as if He owes us something. Yes, He is our Father, and He is responsible for us, but He is also the Almighty God and a consuming fire. The Psalmist describes a 'protocol' for accessing God's Presence. The scripture says, *"Enter his gates with thanksgiving and his courts with praise; give thanks to him and bless his name." Psalms 100:4.*

THANKSGIVING

Gratitude is an excellent conversational ice breaker – remember, prayer is a conversation with your Heavenly Father. Gratitude opens the communication channels and creates room to receive more. An adage goes thus, *"a river that forgets its source will run dry."* By acknowledging Him as our source, we are kept replenished.

Thanksgiving safeguards our minds against the poison of the enemy who tries to flood our minds with thoughts that destroy our faith and cloud our judgement. Such thoughts make us begin to see God as our enemy instead of an ally. We begin to wonder what we have to be thankful for – we recall our losses over our blessings – reminding Him of a lost job, the rent that is due, or even a recent car accident! We then create records and catalogues of events in our lives that have gone wrong, forgetting that, *"for to him that is joined to all the living there is hope: for a living dog is better than a dead lion." Ecclesiastes. 9:4.* Gratitude is the purest expression of our faith, and we know from the Bible that without faith, it is impossible to please God, and if we don't please Him, we cannot secure His help. Losing a battle doesn't mean you have lost the war; there is always hope when there is life.

I sat up one night before my nightly prayers with a paper and pen to write down the things I ought to be thankful for before I prayed. Not knowing where to start, I decided to start from the beginning of my life, so I wrote, *"Father, I thank you for my conception and safe delivery, not all children born on the same day as myself, had the privilege to live to see the first 24 hours of their lives."*

Then I continued rendering prayer points for each year of my life, touching on key events including, academic achievements, career, work, etc. I couldn't finish writing; I was so overwhelmed, with tears running down my cheeks; the realisation of just how good has God has been to me hit home.

In 1897 Johnson Oatman Jnr. published a wonderful hymn that says, *"Count your blessings, name them one by one, it will surprise you what the Lord has done."* The next time your mind wonders about God's goodness, sit back, and take stock of your life, you will be surprised how good the Lord has been.

PRAISE

Now that we have successfully passed through the gates, it is time to enter into His courts with praise. The winning side is always the shouting side. Praise unlocks a unique aspect of God, which invokes His greatness. When His greatness is invoked, His manifest presence is brought into the situation.

I am privy to the testimony of a young man who had a first-hand experience of God's greatness via praises barely 24 hours before his wedding day. According to his testimony, he had no funds to cover certain wedding expenses. He returned home from his Bible school classes, only to be greeted by his distraught aunt, who expected him to come up with funds for the wedding expenses. Since he had nothing to offer, he went into his room to praise God. While he was praising in his room, he heard someone knock the door of his apartment. His distraught aunt refused to answer the door, so he had to leave his bedroom to investigate further.

At the door, he met a lady, who told him that she had heard of the upcoming wedding and presented him with some bags of rice. The groom-to-be was ecstatic; he quickly offloaded the bags of rice into his apartment, and gratefully thanked her. Within himself, he considered that at least he could give his wedding guests uncooked rice as take-home gifts.

He returned to his room, filled with joy, and he resumed his praise to God. His praise was interrupted again by a knock at the door. It was another lady - she was offering her catering services free of charge for the wedding. She asked for the ingredients, and the young man pointed to the bags of rice. She further added that he was not to worry about any other ingredients, including the provision of meat, as she would cover it all. The very thankful prospective groom was on his way back to his room when his aunt asked him what he was doing. He informed her that he was praising God, and she asked if she could join in.

While they were both praising the Lord God, there was another knock on the door; this time the man and his aunt went to see who was at the door. It turned out to be an old school mate of the man. As God would have it, the friend also mentioned that he had heard about the wedding and asked whether a cake had been ordered. The groom advised that there was none – to which the old friend promised to supply the cake for the wedding. True to his word - the next morning, the friend turned up with a seven-tiered wedding cake. Praises caused the hand of God to move here. Praises turned a hopeless situation into a colourful wedding.

I ran across a startling revelation from the following scriptures:

"The king's heart is in the hand of the LORD, as the rivers of water: he turneth it whithersoever he will" Proverbs. 21:1

Praises are pleasing unto God, and when a man's ways please the Lord, He turns the heart of men (or women) toward Him to please Him. You can insist or place demands upon a man or woman, but it is God who gives you favour in their sight; it is Him who makes people go out of their way to see that you are comfortable. Praise is a great tool of deliverance in the hands of a believer. The story of King Saul being tormented by an evil spirit, teaches on the mystery of praises in this light. The scriptures record that an evil spirit tormented the king – but while David sang and played his harp, the evil spirit departed from him without one word of prayers. (1 Samuel 16:14,23).

Praise is not a means to entertain ourselves in church services. We are not the centre of attraction; Jesus is. He said, *"If I be lifted up from the earth, will draw all men unto me."* (John 12:32) The church will begin to grow, and the miraculous will take place when Jesus is lifted high.

Praises give the wings of our prayers to fly. I once heard a preacher say, "Prayer without praise is protest." The spiritual picture we often paint in the prayer room is of a man carrying a placard in his hands, yelling at God to change his mind. Until we create an atmosphere for Him, He cannot be elevated in our situation. So, sing His praises today!

WORSHIP

"But the hour cometh, and now is, when the true worshippers shall worship the Father in spirit and in truth: for the Father seeketh such to worship him." John 4:23

Worship goes beyond singing a slow song in a church service. It is the connectivity of spirits - God's Spirit and man's Spirit. Many have not truly worshipped; as a result, they are spiritually dehydrated. Worship to our spirit is like water to our body; we try to quench our thirst with all sorts of liquids, but none can satisfy. During true worship, we forget who we are and what we are worth; our total attention is on Him, who has made the heavens and the earth. We come humbly before Him in complete reverence and submission.

I was in a church service many years ago; during the worship section of the service, with all hands lifted as an act of total surrender to Him, I paused to adjust my pocket-handkerchief. Immediately I heard the rebuke of the Holy Spirit, "Let no flesh glory in His presence."

"O come, let us worship and bow down: let us kneel before the Lord our maker." Psalms 95:6

We can thank a man for his help, you can praise a man for his skills and ability, but we cannot worship any man, for that would be idolatry. Worship is more of an attitude of the heart than the location we are in. The truth is, you can be in a church building and not truly worship. Not forgetting the reality that our body is the temple of the Holy Ghost.

In worship, we set our priority on God. We shouldn't care what the person next to us thinks about our posture while we worship our God. When reading through the four gospels of the scriptures, it is typical to read about people who sought Jesus for one miracle or the other. They often fell on their faces in worship, and by the time they returned to their feet, they had received their desired miracle.

Worship is a relationship with God that should not only be limited to a Sunday service - after all, none of us has a drink of water only once a week. We can develop our relationship with God through a consistent worship lifestyle that sustains us in times of drought. Often when people seek God, it is because they want something from Him. Worship is not about what we can get from God, but rather ascribing glory to Him. Worship helps us regain our perspective on what truly matters. God is all-sufficient; He doesn't need anyone or anything to make Him 'more' God than He is already. Yet, He seeks true worshippers (John 4:23) because they are in short supply. True worship always requires that we give our very best to God; without Him on our side, the battle of life would be lost, even before it was ever fought.

Stay connected, and you will never run out of supplies.

End of Chapter Prayer Points

All Prayers and Supplications be to the Father in the name of Jesus [John 16:23]

1. Father thank You for the privilege of knowing You as my Lord and Saviour [John 1:12]
2. Father thank You for preserving my life from the noisy pestilence of the enemy [Psalms 91:3]
3. Father thank You for protecting, defending and shielding me from attacks of the enemy [Psalms 127:1]
4. Father thank You for past victories in both visible and invisible battles [Psalms 124:1-2]
5. Father thank You for fortifying Your edge of protection around me and my household with the blood of the Lamb [Revelation 12:11]

1. Oh, Thou that hears prayer, please harken to my voice of supplication today [Psalms 65:2]
2. Father reveal Yourself to me as the ever-present help [Psalms 46:1]
3. Father uproot every seed You have not planted within me, and create in me a clean heart that is holy and acceptable to You [Psalms 51:10; Matthew 15:13]
4. Father teach my fingers to fight and train my hands to war [Psalms 144:1]
5. Father open my eyes to see invisible and secret things I do not know [2 Kings 6:17]
6. Father show me the weakness in the armour of the enemy [1 Samuel 17:48-49]
7. Father remove every filthy garment the enemy is using to gain access into my life [Zechariah 3:3 -4]
8. Father destroy all legalities and evidence mounted against me by the enemy [Revelation 12:10]
9. Father let every strategy and tactic of the enemy against me be turned to foolishness [2 Samuel 15:31]
10. Father reveal to me any weakness in my own spiritual armour [1 Samuel 17:39]
11. Father order my steps so I may not walk into the trap of the enemy [Psalm 37:23]
12. Father every trap and pit the enemy has dug for me, cause them to fall into it with their army [Proverbs 26:27]
13. Father cause the path of my enemy to be slippery and may they fall in their step against me. [Psalm 35:6]
14. Father increase my faith to do the extraordinary and the impossible [Luke 17:5]
15. Father show me wondrous things out of thy Word [Psalms 119:18]

16. Father shine the light of your Word in every dark area of my life [Psalms 119:130]
17. Father disgrace every power of the enemy assigned to disgrace me [Esther 7:10]
18. Lord increase my sensitivity to the voice and leading of Your Holy Spirit [Isa 30:21]
19. Father open my eyes to every deception and distraction of the enemy in Jesus' Name. [Ephesians 4:14-15]
20. Father reveal to me the secrets I need to know in Jesus' Name [Deut. 29:29]
21. Father rain your fire and brimstone in the camp of enemies until they are utterly destroyed [Psalms 11:6]
22. Father destroy every yoke of fear in me that paralyses me in battle against my adversaries [Numbers 13:33]
23. Father arise, let the enemy of my life and destiny be destroyed [Psalms 68:1]
24. Father send your angelic reinforcements to ensure the speedy delivery of my blessings [Daniel 10:12 -13]
25. Father reverse every arrow of the enemy back to the sender, save and deliver all that is mine [Isaiah 49:25]
26. Father cause my enemies to hear strange noises that will cause them to flee into hiding [2 kings 7:3-6]
27. Father strike every evil army assigned against me with blindness [2 Kings 6:18]
28. Father send your angels to release me from every prison in which I have been imprisoned [Acts 12:7 -11]
29. Father let the spirit of sleep and slumber fall onto every enemy of my soul [Romans 11:8]
30. Oh, thou consuming fire, consume the enemy of my soul and destiny [Hebrews 12:29]

1. Father render impotent every weapon of the enemy against my destiny in the Name of Jesus [Isaiah 54:17]
2. Father release upon me the garment of praise in place of the spirit of heaviness. [Isaiah 61:3]
3. Father release upon me the grace to start and finish every project in Jesus' Name [Zechariah 4:9]
4. Father connect me to the constant source of your power [John 15:5]
5. Satan, the Lord rebuke you! [Jude 1:9, Zechariah 3:2]

New Believers' Prayer

You may have read through this book and realised that you are yet to give your life to Jesus. The first step towards our victorious living is to surrender our lives to Jesus and become born again.

It is the most important step you could ever take in life. You can make the decision to live for Jesus today by saying the prayer in this chapter. After this, I recommend that you find a Bible believing church where you can become a member; in order to grow in your relationship with Jesus Christ.

Please do contact me if you need support in locating a church family or even if you just wish to discuss your decision to live for Jesus.

Heavenly Father,

I come to you today as a sinner;
I believe your Word and in your Son Jesus,
that He died on the cross of Calvary
and on the third day He rose again from the dead
for my justification.
Today, I believe and confess
Jesus as my Lord and Saviour,
cleanse me of all my past sins by your blood.
I declare I am born again, thank you Lord
for saving me,
In Jesus name. Amen.

____

Name:

____

Date:

____

Signed:

REFERENCE SCRIPTURES:

If you declare with your mouth, "Jesus is Lord," and believe
in your heart that God raised him from the dead, you will be
saved. For it is with your heart that you believe and are justified,
and it is with your mouth that you profess your faith and are
saved. *Romans 10:9-10*

Therefore, if anyone is in Christ, the new creation has come:
The old has gone, the new is here! *2 Cor. 5:17*

References

1. Derek Prince [1984]. God's Medicine Bottle. United States of America: Whitaker House. P1- 65

2. Sun Tzu [2012]. The Art of War. EMA Publishing. P1 - P46.

OTHER TITLES FROM THE AUTHOR

Becoming One

Unwrapping Your
Redemptive Package